Excel 2019

Charts

EASY EXCEL ESSENTIALS 2019 BOOK 2

M.L. HUMPHREY

ISBN: 978-1-63744-051-3

SELECT TITLES BY M.L. HUMPHREY

EASY EXCEL ESSENTIALS 2019

Excel 2019 PivotTables

Excel 2019 Charts

Excel 2019 Conditional Formatting

Excel 2019 The IF Functions

EXCEL ESSENTIALS 2019

Excel 2019 Beginner

Excel 2019 Intermediate

Excel 2019 Formulas & Functions

ACCESS ESSENTIALS

Access for Beginners

Intermediate Access

CONTENTS

Introduction

The *Easy Excel Essentials 2019* series of titles are for intermediate-level users who want to focus on one specific topic such as PivotTables, Charts, Conditional Formatting, or the IF Functions.

The content of each title is extracted from either *Excel 2019 Intermediate* or *Excel 2019 Formulas & Functions* which cover intermediate-level Excel topics in more detail.

These books are written using Excel 2019 and assuming that a user is working in that program. If you are using an older version of Excel, the *Easy Excel Essentials* series may be a better choice since it was written using Excel 2013 and for a more general audience of Excel users.

With that introduction, let's dive in on how to use Charts.

Charts – Discussion of Types

Charts are a great way to visualize your data. They take a big pile of numbers and turn them into a pretty picture. And, like they say, a picture is worth a thousand words.

I'm pretty good at recognizing patterns if you let me skim an entire data set, but a chart can show what I feel is true (such as that a large percent of sales are coming from one source) with just a few clicks and a big block of color.

Data Format

First things first, your data needs to be arranged properly to create a chart.

Specifically, for most of the charts we're going to discuss, you need one set of labels across the top and one set down the side with values listed in the cells where those two intersect. Do not include subtotals if you can avoid it (you'll have to select around them if you do) and same with grand totals (you'll have to leave them out when you choose your cells). Also, don't include anything in the top left corner of the table where the row labels and column labels intersect.

Here are two examples which would work equally well for this data set.

DATA TABLE OPTION 1						
	201701	201702	201703	201704	201705	201706
Amazon	$100.00	$107.00	$114.49	$122.50	$131.08	$140.26
Createspace	$37.00	$39.59	$42.36	$45.33	$48.50	$51.89
ACX	$23.50	$25.15	$26.91	$28.79	$30.80	$32.96
Con Sales	$10.00			$25.00		$8.00

DATA TABLE OPTION 2				
	Amazon	Createspace	ACX	Con Sales
201701	$100.00	$37.00	$23.50	$10.00
201702	$107.00	$39.59	$25.15	
201703	$114.49	$42.36	$26.91	
201704	$122.50	$45.33	$28.79	$25.00
201705	$131.08	$48.50	$30.80	
201706	$140.26	$51.89	$32.96	$8.00

This is fictitious sales data for each month for various sales platforms. In the first example, the sales channels are listed down the side and the months are listed along the top with the intersection of those two showing the dollar value of sales for that sales channel for that period.

In the second example, each month is listed down the side and each of the sales channels is listed across the top.

How you format your data can impact how your data appears in your charts, especially if you add in a data table which we'll discuss later, so I highly recommend formatting the data in your source table. For example, when looking at my revenue numbers, I don't need to see the cents portion of the value so I usually format my currency entries to remove that.

Alright.

Let's walk through the basics of creating a chart and then we'll discuss the different chart options and what they look like.

Create a Chart

To create a chart from your data, highlight the cells that contain your labels and your values. Remember, do not include any subtotal rows or grand total rows.

If your data is not connected, so you can't just select a single range of values, you can use the Ctrl key to select non-continuous rows or columns.

To do this, select your first range, hold down the Ctrl key, and select your second range. Continue on doing so until all of your data is selected.

Just be sure that each of the selected ranges has the same number of rows or columns so that if they were put together they would form a table with an even number of rows and columns

(The reason this matters is for data integrity, because there's no way to know in your chart whether you're missing results for a particular combination of criteria because it doesn't exist or because you simply didn't select the proper cells. Both will look the exact same in your chart.)

Once you have your data selected, go to the Charts section of the Insert tab and click on the dropdown menu for the chart type you want, and then choose your chart from there. The chart will appear in a new window on top of your worksheet.

Clicking on Recommended Charts in that same section will bring up the Insert Chart dialogue box.

Clicking over to All Charts will show you every available chart type Excel has to offer, listed by category.

If you've selected a set of data that Excel understands (i.e., connected rows and columns) then when you click on Recommended Charts the Recommended Charts tab in the Insert Chart dialogue box will show a handful of charts that Excel thinks match your data. Like this example for our data table on the last page.

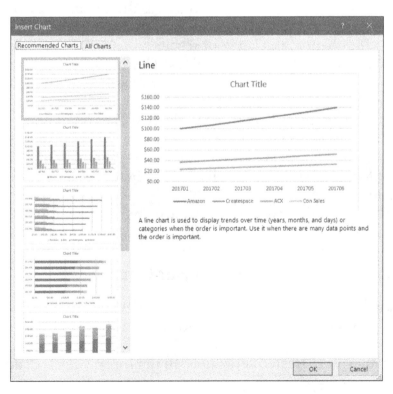

This can be a convenient starting point if you're not sure how you want to display your data. (We will walk through the most common types of charts in a moment after we finish discussing how to create a chart.)

If you're not sure what chart you want, in the Charts section of the Insert tab if you hold your mouse over each chart selection the chart will appear in a separate window so you can easily tell whether it's what you want before you make your selection. But you need to actually click on your selection for it to stay.

Which Chart To Choose

The general rule when choosing a chart is that for time series data like the examples above that include multiple variables (your sales channels) across multiple time periods (each month), the best choices are column charts, bar charts, and line charts.

For data where you have multiple variables but no time component (like total sales for the year), a better choice is a pie or doughnut chart.

Scatter charts are good for random data points where you're looking at the intersection of two or three variables to see if there's any sort of relationship between them.

Histograms allow you to bucket your results so that you can look at how many results you have in a specific range of values. This can often let you see a normal distribution of results, for example, where the majority of the values fall in the center with outliers in either direction.

Excel does offer additional chart types like treemaps, sunbursts, bubble charts and radar charts, but we're not going to cover them in this guide. If you need a chart like that you'll know how it works in general and hopefully our walkthrough of the most common chart types here will let you figure out how to create what you need.

Okay then. Time to discuss Column Charts, Bar Charts, Line Charts, Pie and Doughnut Charts, Scatter Charts, and Histograms in more detail.

Column and Bar Charts

Excel has switched things up a bit for Excel 2019 and now column charts and bar charts are combined under one dropdown in the Charts section of the Insert tab.

(Previously they were treated separately. In the Insert Charts dialogue box they still are. But since they're basically the same thing with the exception that one is horizontal and one is vertical, it kind of makes sense to combine them.)

To create a column or bar chart highlight your data, go to the Charts section of the Insert tab, and click on the dropdown arrow for the top left chart option.

You will then see a dropdown menu with a series of choices. The first two sections are for column charts, the second two sections are for bar charts.

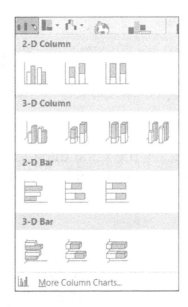

We're going to ignore the 3-D options. They're basically the exact same as the 2-D options just with that three dimensionality (which honestly, truly is probably not needed outside of consulting presentations or annual reports.)

The final 3-D option is a more advanced chart type that creates a three-variable graph, and we're not going to cover that in this guide. (Consider it an Advanced Excel Topic.)

With column and bar charts Excel gives you three choices of chart type. You can choose from clustered, stacked, and 100% stacked.

The clustered option puts the results for each variable (sales platform in the below example) side-by-side for each observation (month in the below example).

You can easily see the height difference between different results, but it can quickly become too busy if you're dealing with a large number of variables.

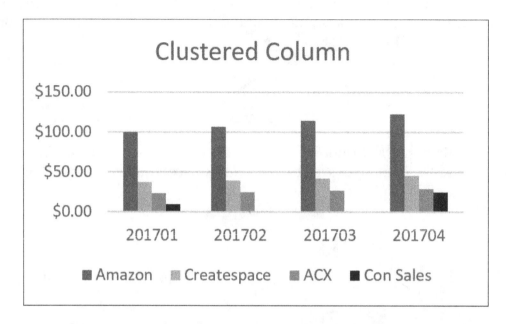

The bar chart version is basically the same thing except the bars are horizontal instead of vertical. The observations move from bottom to top instead of from right to left like in the column chart.

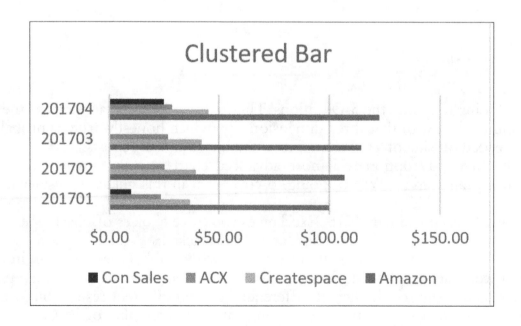

When you have a large number of variables, like I do with my sales channels, then the stacked option is a better choice.

Like with the clustered option, the stacked option has bars of different sizes for each variable based on their value relative to the other values in the chart, but this time the bars are stacked one atop the other instead of shown side-by-side.

So you end up with only one column or bar per time period but you can still identify which one is the largest value based upon the portion of the column or bar it takes up. Like in this Stacked Column chart where Amazon clearly dominates:

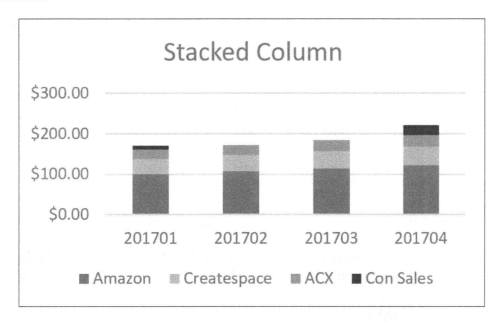

The stacked option is good for showing the overall change from time period to time period.

The 100% stacked option presents all of the information in one column just like the stacked option does. But instead of basing each section's height on its value, it shows the percentage share of the whole which means every single column or bar is the exact same height (which represents 100%).

While you lose any measurement of value (a column chart with values of 2:5:5 will look the exact same as one with values of 20:50:50 or 200:500:500), you can better see changes in percentage share for each variable. (A variable that goes from 10% share to 50% share will be obvious.)

This is an example of the same data as above but in a 100% Stacked Column chart.

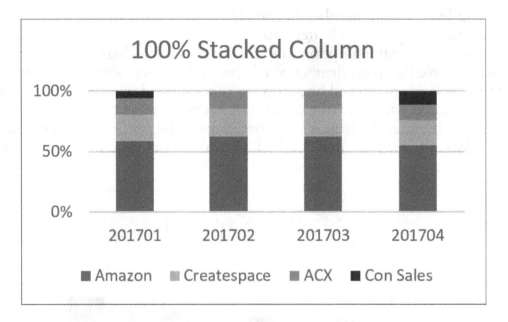

The stacked and 100% stacked bar charts are basically the same as the column chart equivalents except the bars are horizontal instead of vertical.

Line Charts

Line charts are the first chart type shown in the second row of choices. In Excel 2019 they have been combined with area charts, which we're not going to cover.

We're also not covering the 3-D options. And I'm actually only going to cover two of the six 2-D options.

(The other four are meant to do what the stacked columns graphs do and show relative values. I have seen them used by epidemiologists this year to explain data, but I think they're generally counterintuitive unless set up properly with shading under each line.)

So for our purposes all we want are Line and Line with Markers which are the first and the fourth choices.

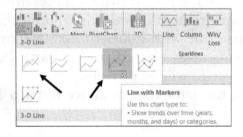

The difference between the line chart and line chart with markers is basically whether there is a point on the line for each observation or not.

Here they are for our data set where we've chosen to chart amount earned per period for four time periods for our four sales channels.

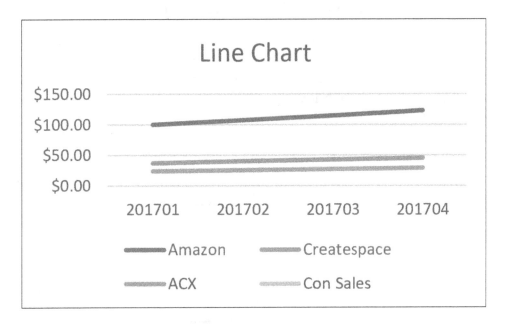

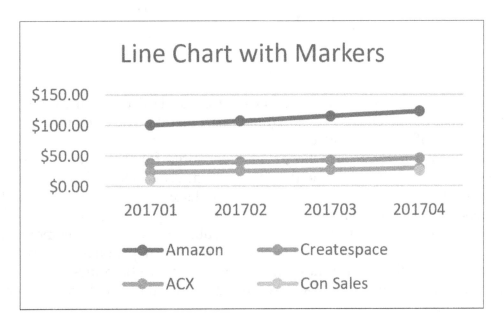

Alright, so that covered the three primary options when dealing with time-series data. But what about data that is all for one time period. For example, sales in a given month or in a given year. That's when the next chart types can be used.

Pie and Doughnut Charts

Pie and doughnut charts are best used when you have one set of observations and want to see the share of the total for each value.

The pie and doughnut chart option is at the bottom on the left-hand side of the chart options. In the dropdown you'll see one 3-D choice as well, but we're just going to use the 2-D ones.

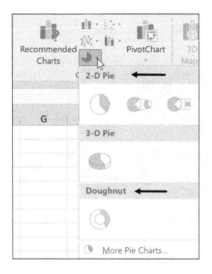

For the pie charts, you can choose between a standard pie chart, a pie of pie chart, or a bar of pie chart. The doughnut chart just has the one option which is the equivalent of the basic pie chart.

If you're only focused on who or what accounts for the biggest share, then use the standard pie chart or the doughnut chart. Each one will assign a section based on relative value for that category. (So share of sales for the period for each sales channel, for example, where the circle is equal to 100%.)

If you want to be able to clearly see the results for all of your segments, even the smallest ones, then the pie of pie chart or the bar of pie chart are potentially better choices. (Although I'm not a fan of either one, to be honest.)

Now let's look at examples. I've used the 201701 data to build each of these.

Here are the basic pie and doughnut chart:

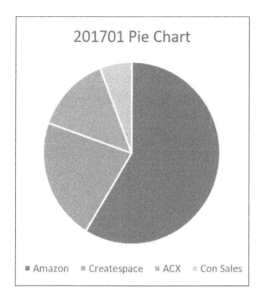

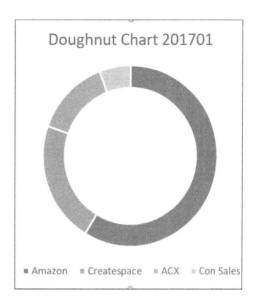

Each chart took the values for a channel (Amazon, CreateSpace, ACX, Con Sales) and assigned it a slice of the pie or circle based upon its relative share ($100, $37, $23.50, and $10) of the whole.

The only difference between the two is that a doughnut chart is hollow in the center.

Now on to the pie of pie charts and the bar of pie chart. Here is an example of a pie of pie chart:

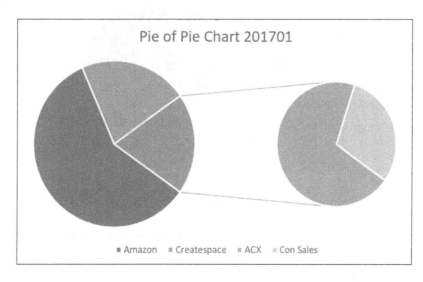

The pie of pie chart creates one main pie chart in which it combines the smaller results to form one segment. Those smaller results are then broken out into another pie chart of their own.

So in the chart above we have ACX and Con Sales that are represented in the main pie chart as one "slice" alongside the other two slices for Amazon and CreateSpace. Those two channels, ACX and Con Sales, are then broken out in their own pie chart on the right-hand side where the size of the slices is base don their value relative to one another. So even though they only represent about 20% of the total between them and Con Sales are only 1/10 of Amazon sales that's not obvious from the way this data is displayed.

The bar of pie chart does the same except it breaks out the smaller results into a stacked bar chart like so:

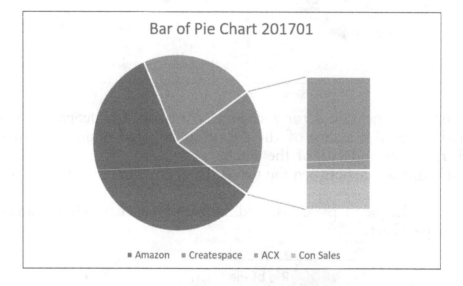

In order to avoid confusion I think the bar of pie chart is probably the better choice of the two since it more clearly distinguishes that it's a subset of data, but honestly I wouldn't use either one if I could avoid it.

(The best charts can be read without explanation and I'm not sure that would be true for either the pie of pie chart or the bar of pie chart for your average user.)

Scatter Charts

Scatter charts (or scatter plots) are the second option on the bottom row of the chart types.

Scatter charts plot the value of variable A given a value for variable B. For example, if I were trying to figure out if gravity is a constant, I might plot how long it takes for a ball to reach the ground when I drop it from varying heights. So I'd plot time vs. distance. From that I could eventually see that the results form a pattern which does indicate a constant. (Thanks high school physics teacher for making physics fun.)

There are five scatter plot options.

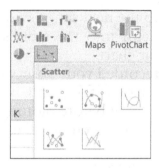

The first one is a classic scatter plot. It takes variable A and plots it against variable B, creating a standalone data point for each observation. It doesn't care what order your entries are in, because there's no attempt to connect those entries to form a pattern.

Here we have some sample height and time values that we've plotted using that first Scatter option. There is a clear pattern to the data that will be much more obvious if we change the chart type to connect those points.

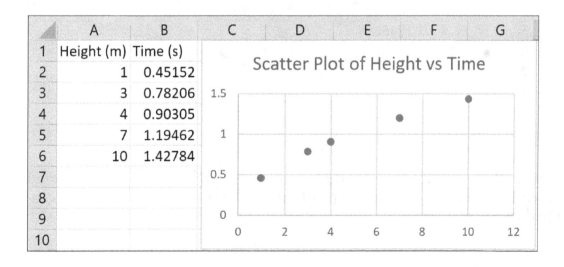

That's where the other four scatter plot options comes into play. They all include lines drawn through the plotted points.

The two smooth line options try to draw the best curved line between points. The straight line options just connect point 1 to point 2 to point 3 using straight lines between each point.

The charts with markers show each of the data points on the line, the charts without markers do not.

Now. One quirk of Excel is that it draws the line from the first set of coordinates in the data table to the next set of coordinates.

This introduces another factor into the table since the order of your data impacts the appearance of your chart.

If the order in which you recorded your observations does not matter, like in this example where it doesn't matter if I drop a ball from 1 meter or 10 meters first, then you should sort your data before plotting it.

In the chart above, because there were no lines to connect the dots whether the data was sorted or not didn't matter. But here's that same data in random order and with a smooth line connecting the data points.

This one has markers so you can still see the curve in the underlying data, but if I were to take those out it would just look like a giant scribble on the page.

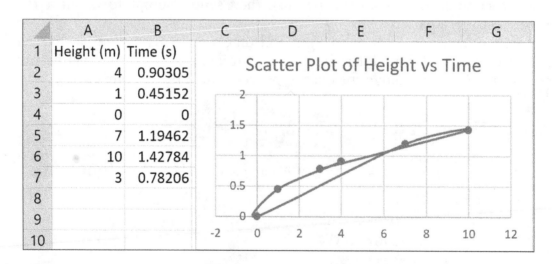

Here is that same data now sorted by height. (I could have as easily sorted by time.) I've used the same plot type of smooth line with markers so you can see the difference.

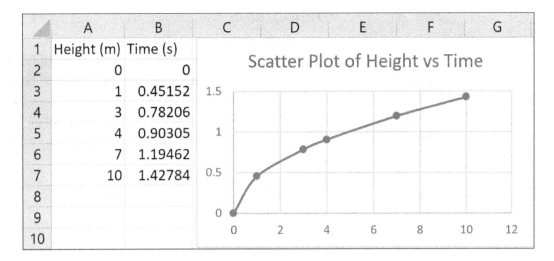

Okay. That was an example with just two data points in it. But you can map multiple sets of data in a basic scatter plot by adding another column of data. The first column will serve as your control value and then the next two columns are the values you're plotting against the control values.

For example, let's say you have sales numbers for two car sales representatives for the first four months of the year and want to compare them to one another.

Here is our data as well as a scatter line plot with straight lines and no markers.

	A	B	C	D
1	**Month**	**Sally**	**Kate**	**Total**
2	Jan	5	15	20
3	Feb	10	12	22
4	Mar	15	7	22
5	Apr	20	8	28

The lines let you clearly see the trend for each of the three categories. Sally is doing better each month, Kate has been doing worse. For the total between them there was a slight increase in the last month measured.

You can technically do a plot like this without plot lines. Each data point will be color-coded, but I don't recommend doing so. It's not near as easy to interpret as the versions with lines connecting related observations.

Histograms

On to one I didn't cover in the original *Intermediate Excel* because it's relatively new but that I think is useful enough that we can cover it here. And that's histograms.

In Excel 2019 the histogram option is located under the center chart choice, Insert Statistic Chart. It is the top choice under that dropdown.

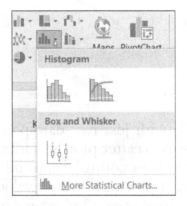

A histogram is perfect for seeing the general distribution of your data results. Rather than plot individual points what it does is buckets your values together into ranges called bins.

So, for example, instead of treating 31, 32, and 33 as separate values a histogram might have a bin for any value between 30 and 39. This can let you more easily see where your values cluster together without getting lost in the minutiae.

Here's our example. I've made up a series of high temperatures for January for a random location similar to Colorado.

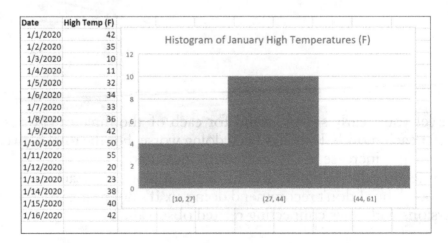

You can see that the range of values has been put in three bins by Excel and that the majority of the values fall into the center bin which contains all values between 27 and 44. The height of each bin is based upon how many values fall into the given range.

(We'll talk next about editing charts. In the chart formatting task pane for a histogram you can set the bin width and/or the number of bins.)

Okay?

Now that you understand the basic chart types, let's talk about how to edit your charts to get them to look exactly like what you want.

Charts - Editing

Chances are, once you've created a chart you'll want to edit it. With the sample charts I showed you in the last chapter I edited the name of each one, resized them, and moved them. But you can do much more than that and we're going to walk through a lot of those options now starting with the Chart Tools Design tab.

Chart Tools Design Tab

The Chart Tools Design tab is only available when you're clicked onto a chart. Once you do so the Chart Tools Design and Format tabs will appear to the right of the Help tab.

We're going to discuss the Design tab and the options on the right-hand side first because these are the ones you can use to fix a chart that doesn't seem to be working the way you expected it would.

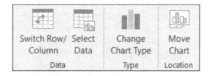

Those options are Switch Row/Column, Select Data, Change Chart Type, and Move Chart.

Switch Row/Column

Once you've created your chart you may find that the data you wanted along the bottom is along the side and the data you wanted along the side is along the bottom. Or even that the data you thought should be in the chart as the results isn't in the chart but is instead along one of the axes.

The first way I try to fix this is by click on Switch Row/Column data. Often that does it. (If that doesn't work then you'll need to consider whether you've selected the correct data and whether the chart type you're using is the right one.)

Select Data

If you realize that the data in your chart isn't what you wanted, you can either delete the chart and start over, which is sometimes the easiest choice if you've done nothing to customize the chart yet.

Or you can go to Select Data and change the data you've selected.

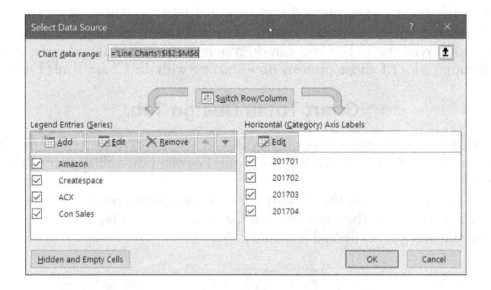

When you click on Select Data this will bring up the Select Data Source dialogue box. You can also see on the screen in the background the selected range of cells that are being used in your chart.

The chart data range at the top shows the selected cells that are being used in the chart. You can manually edit this by clicking into the box with the cell range or edit it by clicking on your worksheet and selecting a new range of cells there.

(I usually use another method for this, which is to click on my chart until I see my selected range of data highlighted and then to click and drag on the square that appears at the edge of the selected range until my new data is also selected.

On my screen those squares are purple, red, or blue and I usually want the purple one that is at the bottom of my left-hand labels. I click and drag down to add more rows of data to the range or drag up to remove rows from the range of data selected.)

If the problem is that you included a category you didn't want to include, like Grand Total, you can also just uncheck that category in the bottom section. For example, under Legend Entries for this table I could uncheck any of the sales channels to remove it from the chart or under Horizontal Axis Labels I could uncheck any of the date values to remove that date range from the chart.

To permanently remove one of the Legend Entries, select it and choose Remove. That will automatically update your data range above as well.

To add a series, you can also click on Add, give the series a name or click on the cell that contains that name already, and then in the series values field select the data to include from your worksheet.

To edit a series under Legend Entries, select the series you want to edit, click on Edit, and then change the selected cells or the name to what you want.

To change the order of the series elements, click on one of the elements and use the up and down arrows.

Change Chart Type

Sometimes you realize that the chart type you chose is the wrong one. Maybe you chose a stacked columns chart and realize that the 100% stacked columns chart is the better option. One way to change to the new chart is to click on Change Chart Type in the Chart Tools Design tab.

That will bring up the Change Chart Type dialogue box with the All Charts tab showing. If you're not sure what you want, you can see suggestions on the Recommended Charts tab that we talked about before. Or you can just select the chart you want from the All Charts tab.

(Another option is to go to the Insert tab and choose a new chart type from there. That will work, too.)

Move Chart

I will confess I never use this. But if you want to move a chart to a new worksheet you can click on that chart and then click on Move Chart and it will give you the option to move the chart to a new worksheet or an existing worksheet in the current workbook.

I usually just select the chart, copy or cut, go to the new location, and paste it.

(We'll talk in a few pages about how to move a chart around within a worksheet, but for now let's finish up with the Design tab.)

The left-hand side of the Design tab (below) is more about the appearance of the chart. I'm going to work from right to left because the left-most option will take an entire page or two to explain.

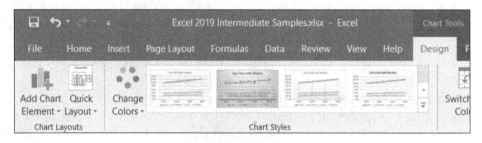

Chart Styles

Excel 2019 provides a number of pre-defined Chart Styles you can choose from.

The number of choices varies depending on the type of chart, but there are usually a variety with different colors and chart elements included or excluded.

In the screen shot above, you can see four examples for a line chart. On the left-hand side of those four options is a scroll bar that will allow you to see even more options.

If you want to see what a style will look like before you choose it, just hold your mouse over it and your chart will update to show the style. Once you find a style you like, click on it and Excel will apply that style to your chart.

I'd say that for me none of the chart styles are ever exactly what I want, but if one is close it can sometimes be easier to select it and then customize from there, especially if you're not quite sure what Chart Element that style is using that gives the chart the appearance you like.

Change Colors

I actually used this for a few of the chart screenshots in the last chapter because the default colors that Excel uses for charts are blue, orange, gray, and yellow and that doesn't always allow for the best contrast when looking at an image in black and white.

We'll talk later about how to change the colors for each item individually to exactly the color you want, but if what you're looking for is a quick and easy option for other color schemes, then Change Colors is the easiest way to get that.

First, click on Change Colors to see the dropdown menu of options. I count seventeen choices. The first few use a variety of colors, the rest use shades of one specific color.

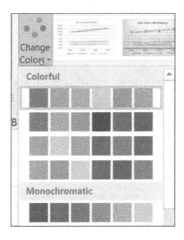

As with Chart Styles you can hover your mouse over each option to see what it will look like. When you find one you like, click on it and Excel will apply it to your chart.

Quick Layout

The Quick Layout dropdown provides a variety of layout options to choose from. The exact number will again depend on the chart type you've chosen.

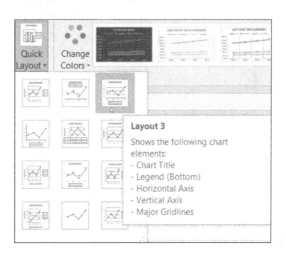

The layouts include various configurations of data labels, axes labels, legends, and grid lines. (One option for scatter charts even includes an r-squared calculation.)

To use a Quick Layout, click on the dropdown and choose the one you want.

Just like with the other quick formatting options, you can hover over each one to see what it will look like before you make your choice. When you do that, as you can see in the above image, it will also list out for you what the different formatting elements are that are being used in that Quick Layout.

If you use a Quick Layout after you choose a Chart Style the color scheme and background colors will stay the same as the Chart Style, but the layout will update. If you choose a Quick Layout and then a Chart Style, the Chart Style will override your Quick Layout, so if you want to combine the two start with your Chart Style.

Add Chart Element

This is the one I use the most. Because I almost always want a data table under my chart so that I can combine the visual chart with the actual results. But there are a lot of other options available here, too.

This is where you go to have more granular control over your axes, titles, data labels, etc.

The options available vary by chart type. If an option isn't available it will be grayed out. For example, Data Table, Lines, and Up/Down Bars are not available for scatter plots.

To see your choices, click on the Add Chart Element arrow. This will bring up a dropdown menu. You can then hold your mouse over each option in the list to see a secondary dropdown menu of available choices.

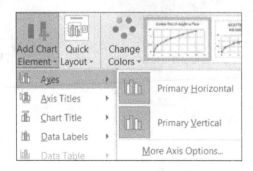

As above, holding your mouse over an option will show that choice on your chart, but you have to click on it to keep it.

If you click on the More Options choice at the bottom of one of those dropdown menus, that will bring up the chart formatting task pane on the right-hand side of the screen which will give you even more control over your charts.

We'll talk about the task pane in a bit. First, let's walk through the options in the Add Chart Element dropdown.

Axes

Axes allows you to add (or remove) the data point labels on each axis.

For example in this chart I clicked on Primary Vertical to remove the vertical axis values which were there by default.

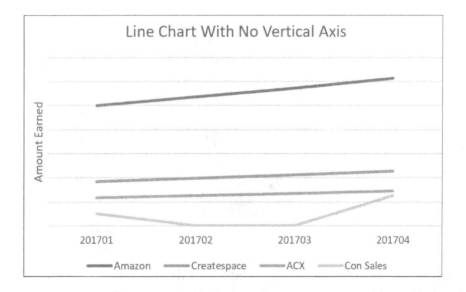

You can no longer see the $ values represented by each line on the chart. You just know that Amazon is much higher than the other lines but not by how much. This could be $5 compared to $1 or $5,000 compared to $1,000.

Axis Titles

Axis Titles allows you to add (or remove) a title for each axis.

In the image above I clicked on Primary Vertical to add a label to the vertical access. I then clicked into the box that was added and changed it to "Amount Earned". The chart above does not have a horizontal axis title.

Chart Title

Chart Title allows you to either (a) remove the chart title entirely, (b) place it at the top of the chart, or (c) place it in a centered overlay position.

All of the examples you've seen so far have the title above the chart.

Data Labels

You can use Data Labels to label each of the data points in your chart.

I find this particularly useful with pie charts and for those will usually choose the Outside End option or the Best Fit option, like below.

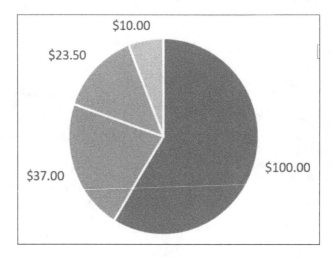

I do sometimes have to click on the labels and drag them to a better location. If you drag them far enough a line will appear connecting the label to its slice.

The default is to show the value, like above, but you can go into the task pane and make that into a percent share instead.

Data Table

Data Table allows you to add or remove a table below your chart that shows the data that was used to create it.

If you're going to do this, you should also at the same time consider removing the legend from the table since you can use the Data Table With Legend Keys option to combine the data table with a legend.

Below is an example of what this looks like with a 100% stacked column chart.

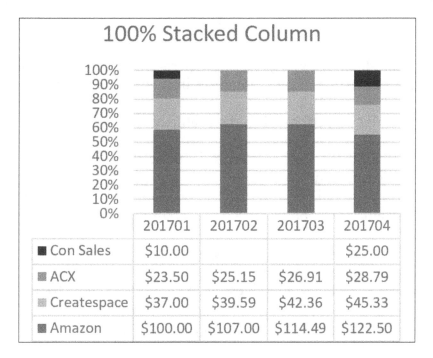

100% Stacked Column				
	201701	**201702**	**201703**	**201704**
■ Con Sales	$10.00			$25.00
▓ ACX	$23.50	$25.15	$26.91	$28.79
▓ Createspace	$37.00	$39.59	$42.36	$45.33
▓ Amazon	$100.00	$107.00	$114.49	$122.50

When you add a data table you will likely have to resize the chart and make it taller to get it to look good. Otherwise it tends to get smooshed up into nothing.

In this example I have added a data table with legend keys, removed the legend that was there, and increased the overall height of the chart.

Error Bars

You can add bars that show the standard error, standard deviation, or percentage error in your data. (Usually you would use these if you had a data set that was predicting values and you wanted to show your potential error range. I wouldn't recommend using these on a chart unless you're dealing with data of that type and know what you're doing.)

Gridlines

The gridlines option allows you to add (or remove) horizontal or vertical lines to your chart. These can make it easier to identify the approximate value of a specific point in the chart. There are Primary Major Horizontal gridlines on the chart above.

Legend

The column, bar, line, pie, and doughnut charts that Excel creates come with a legend which is the listing of the categories in the chart and their corresponding color.

(For the charts we looked at earlier, those little boxes with Amazon, CreateSpace, etc. at the bottom were the legend.)

You can remove the legend using this dropdown like I did above, or you can change its position to right, left, top, or bottom.

If you choose top and bottom, the legend elements will be in a row. If you choose right or left, they'll be displayed in a column.

Lines

Lines allows you to add high-low lines or drop lines to a line chart.

Trendline

You can use Trendline to add a line onto your data to see if it fits a pattern like a linear or exponential relationship. Depending on the data set, you may be limited in your choice of lines you can add. Also, beware of using something like a linear trendline on exponential data. Excel will do it, but it's not the best fit for that sort of data.

Up/Down Bars

You can use this to add Up/Down bars to a line graph if you need them.

* * *

Now that you have all of the elements in place, time to discuss how to change the aesthetics of the chart. Things like size, position, and colors. Some of this you can do directly on the chart in the worksheet and some of it requires using the Chart Tools Format tab.

We'll start with a discussion of what you can do in the Chart Tools Format Tab.

Chart Tools Format Tab

Chart Size

You can go to the Size section on the right-hand side of the Format tab under Chart Tools and specify a width and height for your chart.

Be careful because it doesn't automatically adjust both dimensions. So if it matters that you keep your values proportional, calculate that before you make your change.

I usually use the Size option when I want multiple charts to be the exact same size. Otherwise, I actually change my chart size on the chart itself.

In Excel 2019, if you click onto a chart you've created you'll see white circles appear at each of the corners as well as in the middle of each side. Hover your mouse over each of them and you'll see that the cursor turns into a two sided arrow. If you don't see the two-sided arrow, click on one of the circles and hold your mouse over it again and it should work the second time.

Once you see the two-sided arrow, left-click and drag and you can increase or decrease the size of your chart. Click and drag from the corners to change both horizontal and vertical size at the same time.

With either method, all of the elements within the chart will resize themselves automatically to fit the new size.

Shape Styles

The easiest way to change the color of your chart elements like the bars in a bar chart or pie slices in a pie chart is to use Change Colors.

But if those colors aren't sufficient, you can use the Shape Styles section in the Format tab to change the color of each separate element in the chart one-by-one.

To do so, left-click on the element with the color you want to change. In a bar or column chart all sections that correspond to that category should be selected when you do that. If they aren't try double-clicking.

Also, be careful with pie charts because Excel likes to select all of the slices in the pie, not just that one. If that happens, click on the slice you want one more time and it should select just that slice.

Once you've chosen the element to change, you can click on one of the Shape Styles options which change the fill, outline, and text color. Or you can use the Shape Fill or the Shape Outline dropdown arrows to select a fill or outline color.

Use Shape Fill for bar, column, and pie graphs and Shape Outline for 2-D line graphs.

(If you ever create a 3-D line graph be careful, because if you use Shape Outline you'll only be changing the color on the edges of the line, not the entire line. For those you need to use both Shape Fill and Shape Outline.)

If you use one of the Shape Styles that will automatically be applied to your selected chart element as soon as you click on it. You can hover over each option to see what it will look like before you make your choice.

With Shape Fill or Shape Outline what you will see in the dropdown is a selection of colors as well as the ability to use a custom color with More Color.

With Shape Fill you can also use a picture, gradient, or texture. (Just don't go overboard on that, please. My little corporate soul cringes at the idea of how that could be abused to create truly hideous charts.)

With Shape Outline you can change the weight and type of line used. So you could have a dashed line instead of a solid line, for example.

If you don't like the result, remember to use Ctrl + Z to undo and try again.

There's another option in that section called Shape Effects that allows you to add things like beveling and shadows to the elements in your chart, but I'd encourage you to remember that the central purpose of a chart is to convey information to others and that sometimes adding a lot of bells and whistles gets in the way of that. But you do you.

WordArt Styles

For text in your chart you can apply fancy formatting to the text using the Word Art Styles options. Just select the text you want to format and then choose the WordArt Style you want.

You can also change the text color of text using the dropdown menu next to that which is called Text Fill. (The Home tab formatting options work as well but here you can also apply a picture, gradient, or texture instead of just a solid color.)

In the dropdown after that you can add lines of various widths or patterns around your letters. And in the dropdown after that you can add shadow, glow, reflection, etc. to your letters.

Please use sparingly. I know it's not my business but as someone who has been forced to sit through one too many garish presentations, I have to try.

Edits To Make Within A Chart

As mentioned above, there are some edits you can make directly in the chart. We already talked about changing the chart size that way. Now let's discuss a few other options you have.

Move a Chart

If you want to move a chart within your worksheet, left-click on an empty space within the chart, hold and drag. (You may have to click on the chart once and then click again and hold and drag.)

Don't click on an element within the chart, like the title, because that will just move that element around instead of the whole chart. If you do that, like I sometimes do, just Ctrl + Z to put the element back where it was and try again.

If you want to move a chart to another worksheet or even another file (including a Word file or PowerPoint presentation, for example), you can click onto an empty space within the chart and use Ctrl + C to copy it or Ctrl + X to cut it, and then go to the new destination and use Ctrl + V to paste it there.

Move Elements Within a Chart

You can manually move elements within a chart by left-clicking on the element and then clicking and dragging it to where you want it.

You should see a four-sided arrow when you are able to do this. For fields that can be edited or moved like the various title fields, this may require you to put the mouse along the edge of the field before you can click and drag to move.

Rename a Chart

To change the name of a newly-created chart, left-click on where it says Chart Title to select the title. You should see the title is now surrounded by a box with blue circles in each corner. Click into that box and highlight the existing text, delete it, and then add your own text.

If you're just editing an existing chart name you basically do the same. Click on it to see the box, click into the box, make your edits.

Rename a Data Field as Displayed in the Legend

To change the data labels used in the legend, your best bet is to do so in the data table that's the source of the data in the chart. As soon as you do that, the chart legend will update as well. I mention this here because it can be tempting to assume you can do those changes within the chart and you really can't.

Change Font Properties

If you want to change the font, font color, font size, or font style (italic, bold, underline), another option is to just click on the text element in the chart and then go to the Home tab and change the font options there just like you would with ordinary text in any cell.

Chart Formatting Task Pane

I've alluded to it a few times before, but you may have noticed as you work in your charts that sometimes on the right-hand side an extra box of options appears. This is what I refer to as the chart formatting task pane. There are actually a number of them that appear depending on the chart type and what you clicked on to make it appear.

For example, I'm looking at one labeled Format Plot Area right now. It has that name at the top but right under that is a dropdown menu where I can go to other task panes for that type of chart. Within each of these task panes there are then a few categories of changes that you can make and under each category there are subcategories to choose from that then let you make a series of choices about your chart layout.

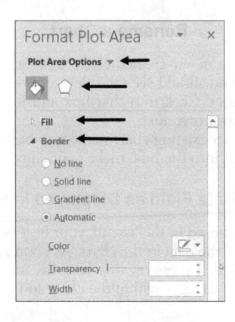

As mentioned before, you can open a task pane by choosing the more options choice for an element under Add Chart Element. Or you can double-click on your chart.

The options you'll be given vary depending on the type of chart and where you've clicked within that chart. You can do things like edit the fill style for chart elements, change the chart border, specify the size of the chart, choose how the text within the chart displays, etc. Basically, all of the things we've already discussed how to do elsewhere. But there are other options that you can only perform in the task pane as far as I know.

For a pie chart this is where I go to change the values shown on the data labels to percentages. (You have to have data labels added already and then it's Label Options, Label Options, and then click on Percentage and unclick Value under that second Label Options section.)

I also come here to "explode" my pie so that there is some space between the pie slices. (Pie explosion is in Series Options, Series Options, and then Series Options again. Move the slider under Pie Explosion to move the slices in the pie apart.)

For a histogram this is where I'd go to change the number of bins or the size of the bins. (Which is under Horizontal Axis, Axis Options, and then Axis Options again. Click on the buttons for what you want to change and the grayed-out values will become editable.)

Basically if there's something you want to do with a chart and you can't figure out where to do it, poke around in the chart formatting task pane.

Conclusion

Alright. That was charts. If you want to learn more niche topics, check out the rest of the series which covers PivotTables, Conditional Formatting, and the IF Functions. Or if you want to now explore a broader range of topics you can choose *Excel 2019 Intermediate* or *Excel 2019 Formulas & Functions* which cover those topics and more.

Appendix A: Basic Terminology

Most of the terminology I use is pretty standard but I think I do have a few quirks in how I refer to things, so be sure to do a quick skim of this section just to make sure we're on the same page. This is meant to be a refresher only. These terms were initially taught in *Excel 2019 Beginner*.

Column

Excel uses columns and rows to display information. Columns run across the top of the worksheet and, unless you've done something funky with your settings, are identified using letters of the alphabet.

Row

Rows run down the side of the worksheet and are numbered starting at 1 and up to a very high number. In Excel 2019 that number is 1048576.

Cell

A cell is a combination of a column and row that is identified by the letter of the column it's in and the number of the row it's in. For example, Cell A1 is the cell in the first column and first row of a worksheet.

Click

If I tell you to click on something, that means to use your mouse (or trackpad) to move the cursor on the screen over to a specific location and left-click or right-click on the option. (See the next definition for the difference between left-click and right-click).

If you left-click, this generally selects the item. If you right-click, this generally creates a dropdown list of options to choose from. If I don't tell you which to do, left- or right-click, then left-click.

Left-click/Right-click

If you look at your mouse or your trackpad, you generally have two flat buttons to press. One is on the left side, one is on the right. If I say left-click that means to press down on the button on the left. If I say right-click that means press down on the button on the right. (If you're used to using Word or Excel you may already do this without even thinking about it. If that's the case then think of left-click as what you usually use to select text and right-click as what you use to see a menu of choices.)

Spreadsheet

I'll try to avoid using this term, but if I do use it, I'll mean your entire Excel file. It's a little confusing because it can sometimes also be used to mean a specific worksheet, which is why I'll try to avoid it as much as possible.

Worksheet

This is the term I'll use as much as possible. A worksheet is a combination of rows and columns that you can enter data in. When you open an Excel file, it opens to Sheet1.

Workbook

I don't use this term often, but it may come up. A workbook is an Excel file and can contain multiple worksheets. The default file type for an Excel 2019 workbook is a .xlsx file type.

Formula Bar

This is the long white bar at the top of the screen with the $f\chi$ symbol next to it.

Tab

I refer to the menu choices at the top of the screen (File, Home, Insert, Page Layout, Formulas, Data, Review, View, and Help) as tabs. Note how they look like folder tabs from an old-time filing system when selected? That's why.

Data

I use data and information interchangeably. Whatever information you put into a worksheet is your data or data set.

Select

If I tell you to "select" cells, that means to highlight them. Same with text.

Arrow

If I say that you can "arrow" to something that just means to use the arrow keys to navigate from one cell to another.

Cell Notation

We may end up talking about cell ranges in this book. Excel uses a very specific type of cell notation. We already mentioned that a cell is referenced based upon the letter of its column and the number of its row. So A1 is the cell in Column A and Row 1. (When used as cell notation you don't need to include Cell before the A1.)

To reference a range of cells Excel uses the colon (:) and the comma (,). A colon between cells means "through". So A1:B25 means all of the cells between Cell A1 and Cell B25 which is all of the cells in Columns A and B and Rows 1 through 25. A comma means and. So A1,B25 would be Cells A1 and B25 only.

When in doubt, go into Excel, type = and the cell range, hit enter, and then double-click back into that cell. Excel will highlight all of the cells in the range you entered.

Dialogue Box

I will sometimes refer to dialogue boxes. These are the boxes that occasionally pop up with additional options for you to choose from for a particular task.

Paste Special – Values

Paste Special - Values is a special type of pasting option which I often use to remove formulas from my data or to remove a pivot table but keep the table it created. If I tell you to Paste Special - Values that means use the Values paste option which is the one with a 123 on the clipboard.

Dropdown

I will occasionally refer to a dropdown or dropdown menu. This is generally a list of potential choices that you can select from if you right-click on your worksheet or on one of the arrows next to an option in the tabs at the top. For example, if you go to the Home tab and click on the arrow under Paste, you will see additional options listed in a paste dropdown menu.

Task Pane

I am going to call the separate standalone pane that appears on the right-hand side of the screen on occasion a task pane. These appear for PivotTables, charts, and the Help function.

About the Author

M.L. Humphrey is a former stockbroker with a degree in Economics from Stanford and an MBA from Wharton who has spent close to twenty years as a regulator and consultant in the financial services industry.

You can reach M.L. Humphrey at:

mlhumphreywriter@gmail.com

or at

www.mlhumphrey.com